The PEARLS

of

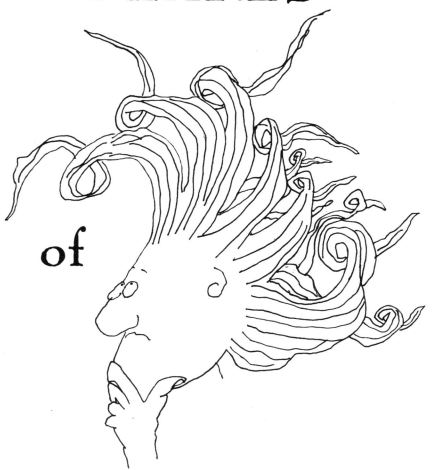

WISDUMB

Goofy Guru Publishing presents . . .

The PEARLS of WISDUMB

The Electric Light Verse
and Shocking Scribbles of
Mozzzzz...

Goofy Guru Publishing
Alice "Apple" Apel, Editor-in-Chief
405 Kiowa Place, Boulder, CO 80303, USA
goofygurupress@attbi.com
www.goofyguru.com

Design by Jane Raese

An enormous arigato to Lynn "Lady Lingo" Arts,
and a mega mozz-nod 'n' salute t' Shel.

Library of Congress Control Number: 2003101390
ISBN 0-9726130-0-5

Printed in China
Third printing

for Cassia and Brett

Open this odd oyster . . .

Step into its world,
Become a goofy guru
Through the wisdumb of the pearls.

THE FIRST LESSON OF LIFE

"Isn't the sky so like the sea,
The most beautiful blue you've ever seen?"

"Yes, indeed, that much is true.
But here's a little surprise for you.
For if you dip your toes in the sky,
It's really rather nice and dry."

T-SHIRT TATTOO

Do you know what I'd like to do?
Go and get a tattoo—
Perhaps an anchor, an eagle,
Or a dragon in greens and blues.

But instead of it on my skin,
I think I'll have it on my shirt.
That way my mom won't mind,
And also, it won't hurt.

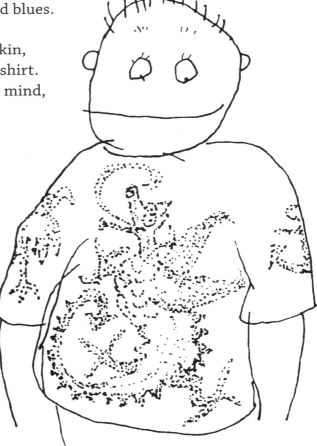

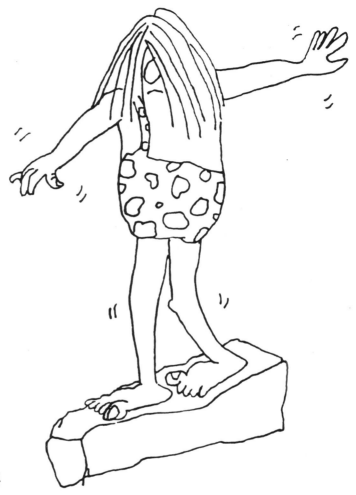

SLOW SKATING

"You know, in the Stone Age they had skateboards."
"Really? Are you sure?"
"Yes, but back then they had little appeal
'Cause they still hadn't invented the wheel."

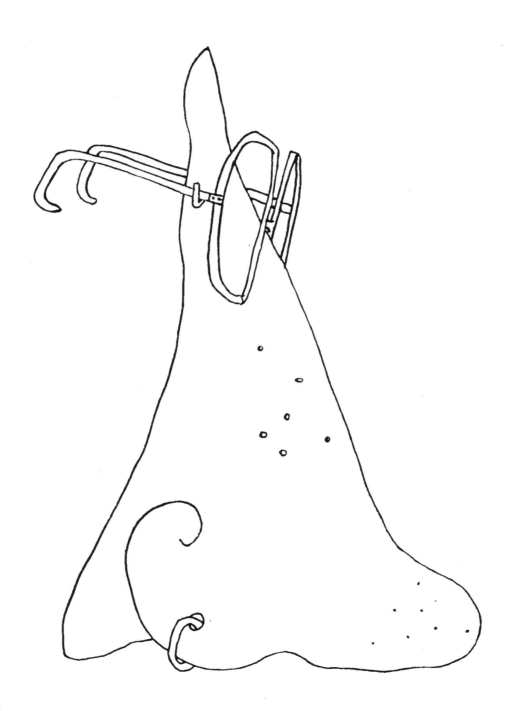

GOD NOSE

On the island of Nostralia
They worship a giant nose.
To you it might seem silly,
But no one's ever caught a cold.

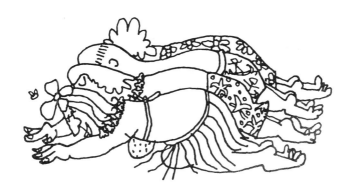

RAPID REPTILE

My tortoise is not so slow.
In fact, he can really go
Faster than the speed of light,
Or nearly, I suppose.

He can do the hundred meters
In about ten seconds flat.
And I bet you're wondering,
"How can a tortoise do that?"

Well, being a professional tortoise trainer,
And a very good one, too,
I can't really tell you,
But I'll give you a little clue . . .

FREEDUMB
(Ode to a classroom fly)

Circling up high—
A solitary fly.
And looking up at it,
I talked to it in my mind.

Are you here to learn,
To seek the powers of knowledge?
Are you hoping to graduate
And study garbology at college?

Or are you here to mock?
To giggle and to laugh?
And pull all sorts of faces
At all of us in class?

But obviously it was unaware
Of the questions that I posed,
Up there in the air—
Busy buzzing, I suppose.

It simply flew in circles,
Completely ignoring me,
As brainless as a baseball bat
But absolutely free.

IF YOU CATCH A DRAGON

If you catch a dragon in your net,
And it roars, "PLEASE, LET ME GO?"
Roar back, "NO!"

"How about if I give you my weight in gold?"
If the dragon tempts you so,
Simply say, "NO!"

Or if the dragon's eyes all fill with tears,
And he cries, "OH, PLEASE, MAY I GO HOME?"
Cry out, "NO!"

But if the dragon bellows and roars
While sheets of flame pour from his jaws,
And in your net he burns a giant hole and goes,

"YOU LITTLE CREEP,
WHAT DO YOU MEAN 'NO'?
NOW, CAN I GO?"

Then I guess . . . I guess . . . I guess . . .
I guess you should say, . . . "YES!"

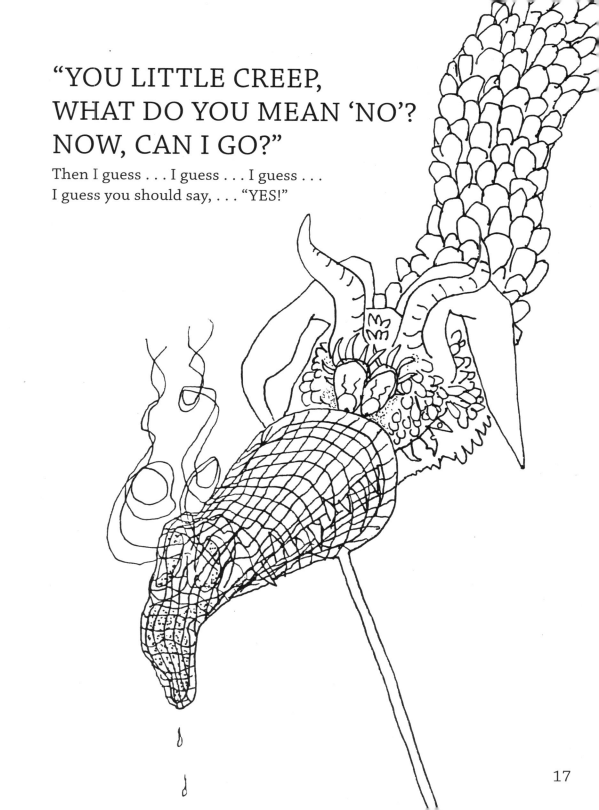

THE TROUBLES OF A TIGER TUNER

I'm a tiger tuner,
I'm a wolf whistler,
I'm a porcupine juggler.
I'm a shark shooter,
I'm a snake swallower,
I'm a tarantula trainer.
I'm a scorpion stroker,
I'm an alligator waiter.
I'm a piranha charmer,
I'm a swordfish fencer,

And . . .
I was wondering if
You were going to be free,
So while on vacation
You'd fill in for me?
Only for a week!
What do you mean, "EEEK!"?
Well, four or five days—
No? I'm really amazed!
OK then . . . how about a couple of hours?
Not even a second?

Huh—some friends are just cowards!

I SHRINK, THEREFORE I AM

When my mom washes my shirts,
She has the habit of making them shrink,
But I'm a little worried this time—
Could it be me who's shrunk, you think?

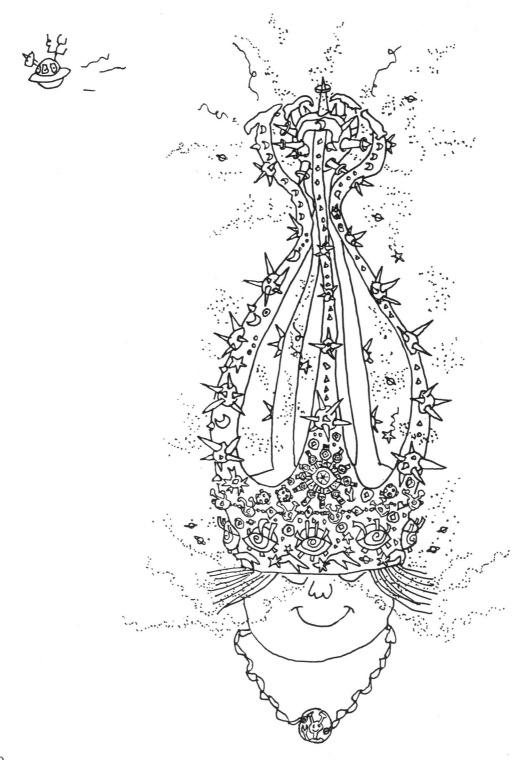

KING OF THE GALAXY

Only when I daydream, I reckon,
When I look out the classroom window for a split second . . .
Only when I lose my concentration,
When I use my vivid imagination,
Do I find myself, it seems
Crowned King of the Galaxy.
Where every command is instantly answered
By "Yes, your Majesty, Oh Master."
When I say, "Do all my homework for me,"
And my servants comply with every need.
Or I say, "Let there be playtime for eternity,"
And they bow down on one knee, "As you please, your Majesty."
And, "Make sure my grades are the best in the class,
Erase all the bad ones from the past,
Bring me the royal jet instead of that old school bus,"
And it's done without a fuss.
Oh, it's only when I daydream, I reckon,
When I look out the classroom window for a split second . . .
When I lose my concentration,
And use my vivid imagination,
Do such scenes and schemes become a reality,
And I'm crowned King of the Galaxy.

FLYING FURNITURE

A flying carpet travels at an incredible speed,
Whisking you quickly from A to B.
But unfortunately it tends to slow down a bit
When you have all your furniture piled up on it.

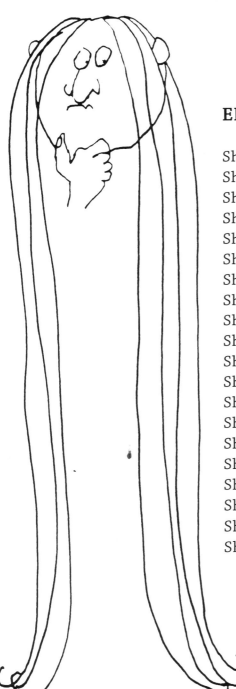

ER...?

Should he cut his hair?
Should he grow it to his feet?
Should he part it on the left?
Should he keep it very neat?
Should he dye it pink and vivid green?
Should he comb it back and grease it down?
Should he clip it closely by his ears?
Should he brush it forward from the crown?
Should he pile it up into a quiff?
Should he keep it under a wooly hat?
Should he iron it straight or try it curly?
Should he get it nibbled by a rat?
Should he go in for the porcupine look?
Should he perm it into flowing waves?
Should he twist it up into a point?
Should he always have a style-a-day?
Should he weave it into a thousand braids?
Should he shear it very close behind?
Should he snip it into animal shapes?
Should he let it fall into his eyes?

Should he knit it into a hairy scarf?
Should he sweep it into a towering spire?
Should he drape it all in twinkling lights?
Should he have long pigtails all on fire?
Should he have it shaggy like a dog?
Should he tuck it all behind his ears?
Should he let the birds come and nest in it?
Or . . .

Should he go for
something weird?

Should he coat it all in icing sugar,
  put cherries round the sides?
Should he add some decorations,
  perhaps at Christmas time?
Should he shave his girlfriend's name
  right across the top?
Should he paint it all in stripes
  or perhaps in spots and dots
Should he have it all in patches,
  crisscrosses and little squares?
Or . . .

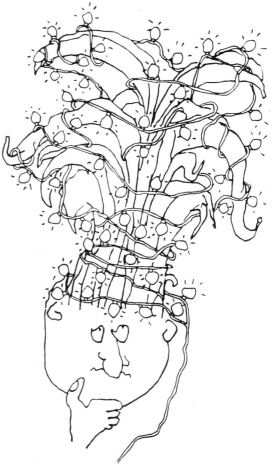

Should he
    use
  the glue
    and pin
      it up,
        miles
          into
            the
            air?

Should he clip it? Grow it? Curl it? Shave it?
Wax it? Oil it? Brush it? Burn it?
Tie it? Twist it? Style it? Leave it?
Dye it? Daub it? Comb it? Quiff it?
Spike it? Knit it? Flick it? Shape it?
Paint it? Glue it? Pin it? Bake it?
Perm it? Press it? Spray it? Wave it?

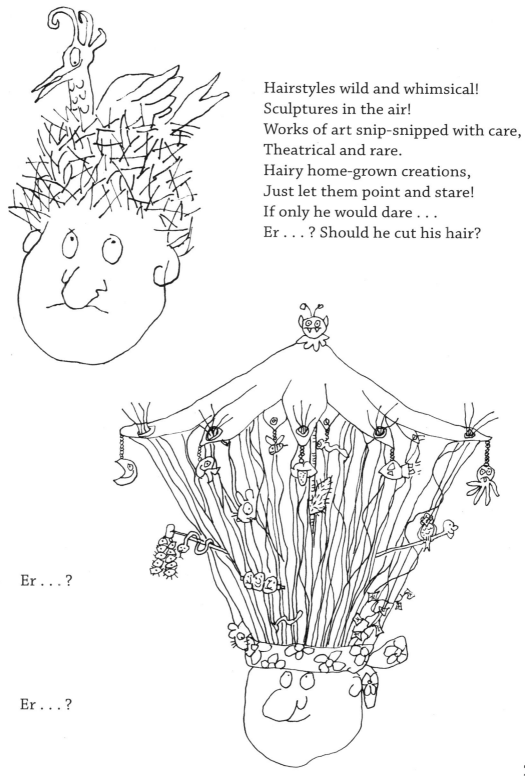

Hairstyles wild and whimsical!
Sculptures in the air!
Works of art snip-snipped with care,
Theatrical and rare.
Hairy home-grown creations,
Just let them point and stare!
If only he would dare . . .
Er . . . ? Should he cut his hair?

Er . . . ?

Er . . . ?

27

Er . . . ?

Er . . . ?

Always er . . .? and er. . . ? and er . . . ?
Never to decide at all.
But of course, it doesn't matter any more
'Cause I'm afraid to say . . .

. . . he's bald!

DOME COMB

Of course, he still takes
    pride
In looking nice and neat,
Using his special comb—
The one without the teeth!

POOR PLOP

I
Pity
The
Poor
Raindrop,
When
It
Wants
To
Stop,
But
Finds
Out
Much
Too
Late,
That
Raindrops
Don't
Have
Brakes.

INDEPENDENT YO-YO

Spiders make excellent yoooooo-yoooooooooos.
Up and down they gooooooooooooo,
But watch out for the spider
With a mind of its ooooooooooooooown!

31

BUSTED BOARD

There's something wrong with this surfboard.
It's stopped. It won't go.
How come it was okay on the sea
But not upon the road?

LET THE HAT STAND SIT

I think you should let the hat stand sit,
Let the sitting room stand.
Let the window box,
Let the radio play,
Let the electric fan have your autograph.
Let the fruit bowl,
Let the key ring,
Let the light bulb put on some weight.
Let the handkerchief rule,
Let the milk shake,
Let the armchair have legs too.
Let the carpet really be a pet,
Let the cat flap,
And you might as well let the wrist watch.

But I really don't think
You should let the kitchen sink.
(Well, not when I'm in it!)

HAPPINESS

Happiness is a finger,
Coming down the road,
And to its great delight
Meets a friendly nose.

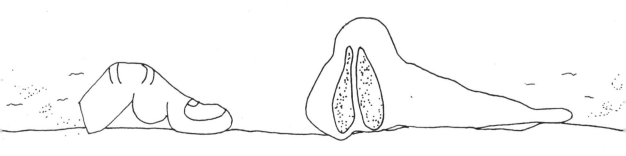

SUPERSONIC GRANNIE

Going through the park
Wasn't that much fun,
Especially when
Her walking stick
Decided
To run.

DINOSAURS AND I DON'T MIX

I'm allergic to dinosaurs.

They make me break out
In spots and sores.
They give me warts,
A rash of pimples,
Unitchable itches.
Premature wrinkles,
Purple blotches,
Bleary eyes,
Screaming shivers
Down the spine.
A furry tongue,
A frothy mouth.
I bare my fangs,
My hair drops out,
My nose clogs up,
My stomach churns.
My toes all curl.
I run around,
I scratch the cat,
I bite the dog,
Because of that
Quite simple fact—
Dinosaurs and I don't mix.

I don't want them snuggling or giving me licks.
I don't want them in my house at all.
I don't want them walking through my walls.
So, please, for the sake of my allergy,
Keep your beast on its leash!

PET POEM

"Mousy" Morris, our science teacher,
Has a really squeaky voice,
And sometimes it's hard to hear him
Over all the classroom noise.
But I heard him say quite distinctly
That we could bring in a few of our pets,
'Cause maybe some of us would like to be zoo keepers or vets,
And we could talk about all the different animals—
Where they come from, and what they eat.
And everyone was so excited and thought that was real neat.

So Roger Skinnywithers brought in his pet toad.
Ugly but cute, I suppose.
It had the delightful habit
Of disappearing into people's clothes
(like down the back of Hillary Willowby's dress—
That was lots of fun, I must confess).
And Susie Richards brought in "Wolfman,"
Her great big fluffy dog,
That looked like it had just had
A high-voltage electric shock.
And it howled like in those horror films,
When there's a full moon in the sky,
And we were all so scared we hid under our chairs,
And all you could see were our eyes.

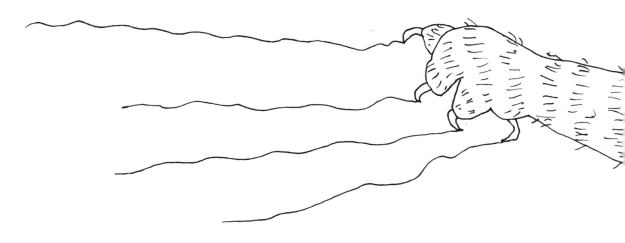

But it was what happened next
That I personally liked the best.
It was when I introduced my cat to the class,
And everyone gave a little gasp.
For my cat is no ordinary feline friend,
No little ball of ribbon and hair,
But rather the mammoth kind of creature—
A mega-meowing purring bear.

And when I took him out of his box,
Wolfman immediately stopped howling,
'Cause he knew he couldn't compete
With the magnitude of the meowing.

But in a way, I knew I shouldn't have brought him.
When I think of ol' Mousy Morris's voice,
I should have brought Speedy, my pet snail—
My cat was certainly the wrong choice.
But I suppose it's too late now
To turn back the clock.

I suppose it's too late now
For the cat to go back in the box.
T'was too late after ol' Mousy spoke,
And my cat pricked up his ears,
And listened to that squeaky voice
    of Mousy's . . . oh, dear!

Well, to cut a long story short,
You'll be glad to hear that ol' Mousy
    didn't get caught,
Although the ensuing chase was
    quite a sight,
With our teacher eventually dangling
    from the light,
And a 10-ton cat sitting underneath,
Smiling up with all his teeth.

And, you know, we never did get
    to talk about
Where different animals come from
    or what they like to eat.
(Although we had a pretty good idea
    from viewing my ol' cat's teeth.)
Nor did we ever get to talk about
    zoo keepers and vets,
And I don't think we ever will,
'Cause I'm sure that's the very last time
We'll be able to bring in our pets.

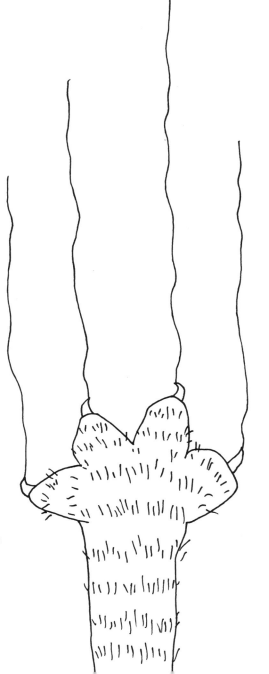

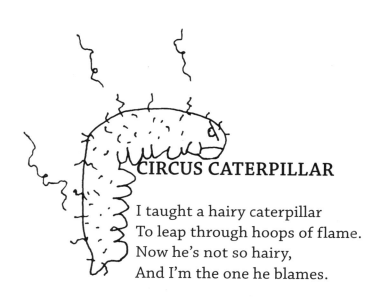

CIRCUS CATERPILLAR

I taught a hairy caterpillar
To leap through hoops of flame.
Now he's not so hairy,
And I'm the one he blames.

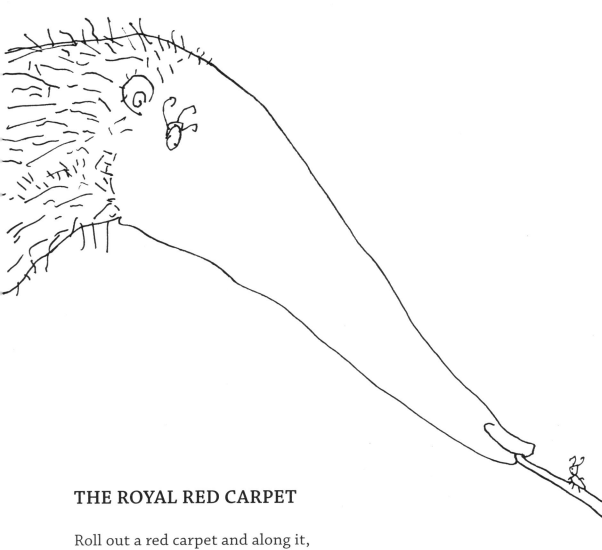

THE ROYAL RED CARPET

Roll out a red carpet and along it,
In regal procession, ants will come.
But far from being regal, I'd say they were just plain dumb,
Not knowing the difference between a carpet and a tongue.

THE BOING BIRD

The Lesser Spotted Boing Bird
Doesn't fly by wings,
But is launched into the air
By a pair of natural springs.

How novel, you're thinking,
How inventive, how handy.
But you're not a Boing Bird
Who's thinking of landing.

BOOMERANG BILL AND BOOMERANG BETTY

For poor ol' Boomerang Bill
Life's a circular track.
When he thinks he's going out,
He's really coming back.

      Every couple of minutes
      He gets up from his chair.
      Once around the room,
      And again he's sitting there.

The world might wake up on Friday
To greet the dawn's first light,
But poor ol' Boomerang Bill
Has returned to Thursday night.

The book that Boomerang's reading
Will never have an end,
For after the very last page,
He turns to the front again.

His wife, ol' Boomerang Betty,
Doesn't seem too much better.
She's been doing the same ol' thing
From the first day that he met her.

She'll cook his favorite dinner
And bring it proudly in,
Pass it by his nose,
Then throw it in the bin.

"Good night, Bill," she'll say,
As she snuggles into bed,
Then turns the other way
To kiss the wall instead.

Last month they planned to go
To a hot exotic spot.
They got in the car and drove
Just around the block.

"I'm leaving you," says Betty.
"I'm leaving too," says Bill.
But come tomorrow, come next year,
I'll bet they're together still.

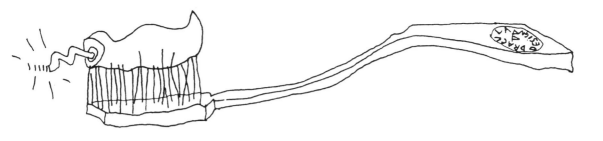

DYNABRIGHT

Brush y' teeth up and down,
Brush y' teeth with gargling sounds.
Brush y' teeth left and right,
Brush y' teeth day and night.
Brush y' teeth with superhuman power,
Brush y' teeth while in the shower.
Brush y' teeth under the moon,
Brush y' teeth in the living room.
Brush y' teeth when going to school,
Brush y' teeth in the swimming pool.
Brush y' teeth at the back of the bus,
Brush y' teeth before they rust.
Brush y' teeth in the pouring rain,
Brush y' teeth on a runaway train.
Brush y' teeth at every o'clock,
Brush y' teeth in only y' socks.
Brush y' teeth back and forth,
Brush y' teeth on a galloping horse.
Brush y' teeth with electric machines,
Brush y' teeth in y' dreams.
Brush y' teeth while playing the harp,
Brush y' teeth in the dark.
Brush y' teeth with all y' might,
Brush y' teeth with dynamite.
Now y' teeth y' can ignore—
Y' won't have to brush them anymore.

TO BEE OR NOT TO BEE

Last night I had a nightmare
Where I found myself changed into a giant bee
(As strange as it may seem).
But in the mirror this morning, I'm glad to see
That luckily it was only a dream.

THE WAY TO NOWHERE

When I asked the way to Nowhere,
They said, "It's somewhere over there.
Over the mountains of Me and You,
Through the swamps of Which to Choose,
Into the Jungles of Gibberish
And left at the corner of Oh, I Wish.
But beware of the dreaded Tru-Tru Tribe
Who tell the greatest big white lies.
Go into the Wood That's Misunderstood,
Straight on through the Land of Should,
Across the bridge to I Told You Town,
Down Whoops Street where you'll hear the sound
Of the yaps of the terrible Tittle-Tat Tongues,
Who beat upon their tommyrot drums.
But take some mud and plug your ears
And travel through the Far and Near
By the raging river What's Going On,
That to some is more than a lifetime long.
Eventually you should reach a sea
And spy the island What May Be.
Dive in and swim against the tide,
And leave your memories all behind.
Swim faster than the Dumb-Dumb Fish
Until you meet the Shores of If.
Here you'll be greeted by the Baffled King,
Who won't seem to know a single thing
About who you are or why you're there.
So he'll pass you on to I Don't Care,
The Queen of So What, who will lead
You on and on through the Puzzled Trees.

At last she'll point and push you through
A hole with a signpost 'I Wish I Knew,'
And down you'll float through foggy air
But Nowhere will be nowhere there.
Instead it should be just due west,
So take a little well-earned rest.

Then climb the mountains of Me and You,
Wade through the swamps of Which to Choose,
Into the Jungles of Gibberish,
And left at the corner of . . ." Oh, I wish
I'd never asked the way to Nowhere,
That's somewhere over there.

UNDERWATER ENVY

Eric, the electric eel,
Is the envy of the sea,
Being the proud owner
Of a waterproof TV.

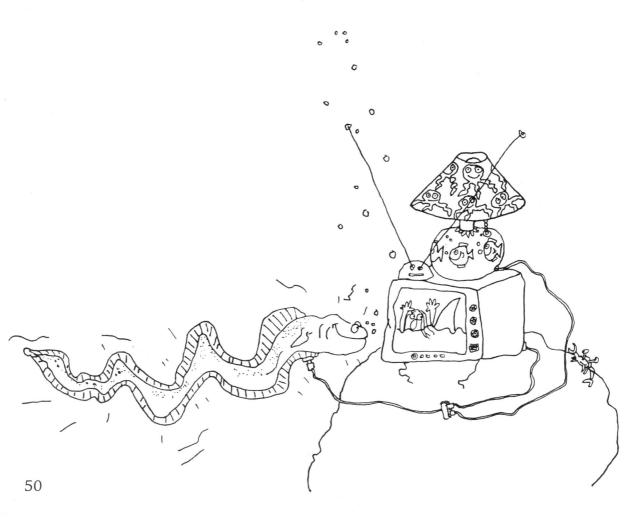

SEA YOU

When octopi pass each other by,
They simply nod or wink an eye
'Cause they really haven't got time to stand
And politely shake a bunch of hands.

SWALLOWMAN

Every year, when the weather gets chilly,
He starts to act extremely silly.
Perching upon the roof,
Hanging from the telephone wires,
Popping flies into his mouth,
Asking people, "Hey, which way is south?"

Oh, the urge, the urge to be a bird
Is indeed so very strong.
He hops around the garden
And bursts out into song.

And when at last the day arrives,
When feathered friends take to the skies,
Off to distant exotic shores
Where everything's sunny and snuggy warm,
Poor ol' him is left right there,
Looking longingly into the air,
Flapping his arms up and down,
Chirping, "Come back fellas! Hey, wait for me!"
As they disappear above the trees.

But deep down in his human heart,
Try as he may to be a swallow,
He knows he's not and so must stand and watch,
Yet sadly never follow.

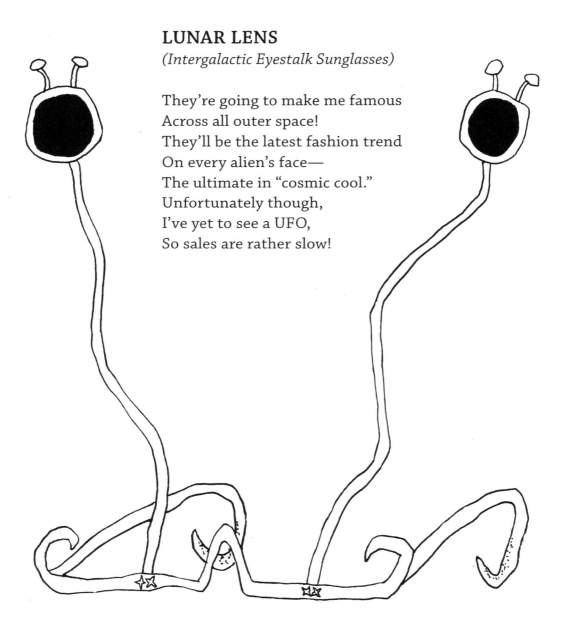

LUNAR LENS
(Intergalactic Eyestalk Sunglasses)

They're going to make me famous
Across all outer space!
They'll be the latest fashion trend
On every alien's face—
The ultimate in "cosmic cool."
Unfortunately though,
I've yet to see a UFO,
So sales are rather slow!

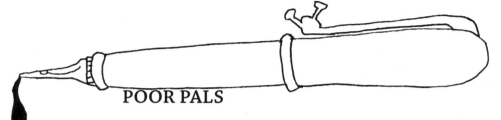

POOR PALS

I thought that having a pen pal
Was being a pal to a pen,
And I've really tried to be a friend—
A pal to every pen.
But sadly, always, in the end
The pens that I befriend
(Johnny's, Jenny's, Robbie's, Al's)
Have shown me categorically
That we cannot be pals.
For if I go and smile at one
And give a friendly wink,
All it does is turn on me
And cover me in ink.

THE MUSIC OF ANGELS

On Thursdays we have music lessons
With Ollie Octave, our music teacher,
Who tells us to open up our mouths
Like gaping deep-sea creatures

And breathe in a great gulp of air,
Deep into our lungs.
Then to let it out so very sweetly
On our little angel tongues.

And of course, we always try to comply
By opening wide our mouths
And letting out that gulp of air
In a scale of sugary sounds.

But instead of little lilting melodies
And beautiful angelic tunes,
Comes a chorus of cats with their tails in a trap—
An ear-bending sonic stew.

A row of crows on the telephone line,
Violins played with a saw,
Screech owls in a tunnel,
Elephants when they snore!

Oh, poor ol' Ollie Octave,
Sometimes I pity him so,
Especially when we sing so sweet
And break the classroom windows.

THE KING AND PIE

Four and twenty blackbirds
Baked in a pie,
Two hundred and sixty turtles
Popped in a pot.
Half a dozen weasels
Rolled and fried in flour,
A score of sleeping dormice
Bubbling and hot.

When the pie was opened,
Ladled on a spoon,
Scooped out of the pan,
A wriggling steaming stew,
They all began to shriek and squeak,
To whistle and to sing.
Not much of a dainty dish
To set before a king!

But the king, he put a turtle
Into both his ears,
Then tucked into his dinner:
"Umm . . . tasty—but weird!"

INFLATABLE PHANTOMS

D' y' wanna buy one of these scary balloons?
It'll make y' mom jump out of her skin.
And I'll tell y', it's even scarier
If you pop it with a pin!

THE BIG ABOMINABLE WORDEATER

The Big Abominable Wordeater spends his life at dinner,
Stuffing his jaws with words and not getting any thinner.
Plump and juicy sounds dribble from his mouth
And roll upon his tongue that flickers in and out.
"Succulent" and "luscious," "oozy," "squashy," "ripe"—
Words to gnaw and chomp, suck and crunch, and bite.
Round, delicious words like "sugary," "slurpy," and "yummy."
Words that stick to fingers: "gooey," "gluey," and "gummy."
Words to chew and chew: "eternal" and "forever."
Ones with high IQs: "brainy," "smart," and "clever."
Words that try to get away: "squiggling," "squirmy," and "wormy."
Words of savory shapes like "conical," "bendy," and "curly."
Long, long-lasting ones such as "marathon" and "mile."
And the ones that are his favorites—"giggle," "chuckle," and "smile."

The Big Abominable Wordeater devours libraries for his lunch,
Volumes of encyclopedia disappear in one great munch!
You can find him in a bookshop, perhaps in the Cookery Section,
Where he finds all those glossy pages are done to perfection.
He likes to down a dictionary or swallow a magazine rack,
Or nibble on a newspaper or a paperback for a snack.

Yet the Big Abominable Wordeater has never had enough.
He's always on the prowl for more of the wordy stuff.
A bookshelf in a bedroom, a comic on a chair—
He's not particularly fussy, he doesn't really care
What and when and where he eats his fill of words,
Although a piece of poetry is something he prefers.
So . . . silently turn the page—can you hear him licking his lips?
Go on, read on a bit—but do it at your own risk!

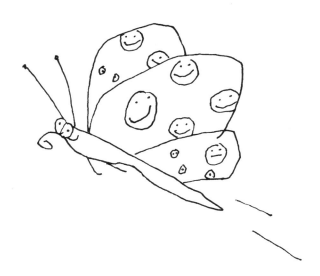

FUTURE FLIGHT

"Oh," said Madame Moon, "I can see a great change in your life."
"I see nectar . . . nets . . . flowers . . . flight . . ."
"Flight? Are you all right? How do you expect a guy like me to fly?"
"Umm . . . ," thought the caterpillar. "What a load of lies!"

61

SURPRISE PRIZE
(not to be read but to be roared)

I SUPPOSE IT'S RATHER NICE
TO BE APPRECIATED AT LAST.
LOOK! I'VE RECEIVED A PRIZE,
"THE LOUDEST VOICE IN CLASS."
NATURALLY I SHOULD FEEL PROUD,
AND I KNOW I SHOULDN'T COMPLAIN,
BUT I REALLY WOULD HAVE PREFERRED
GETTING "BEST AND BIGGEST BRAINS."
BUT ALL RIGHT, OK, NEVER MIND—
I SUPPOSE THIS ONE IS FINE
ALTHOUGH IT'S STILL A BIG SURPRISE . . .

WHY THIS PRIZE?

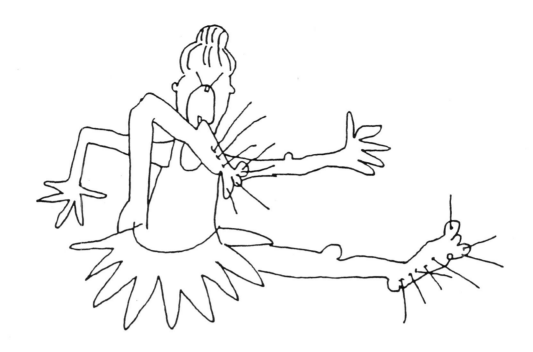

PRICKLY PIROUETTE

She really was the most amazing dancer,
With a style that was one of a kind.
And people would wait in long, long lines
To see her dance her masterpiece
In the Ballet of the Porcupines!

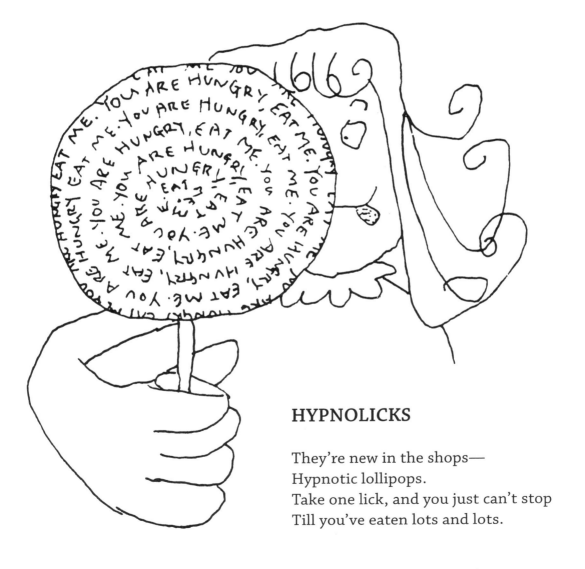

HYPNOLICKS

They're new in the shops—
Hypnotic lollipops.
Take one lick, and you just can't stop
Till you've eaten lots and lots.

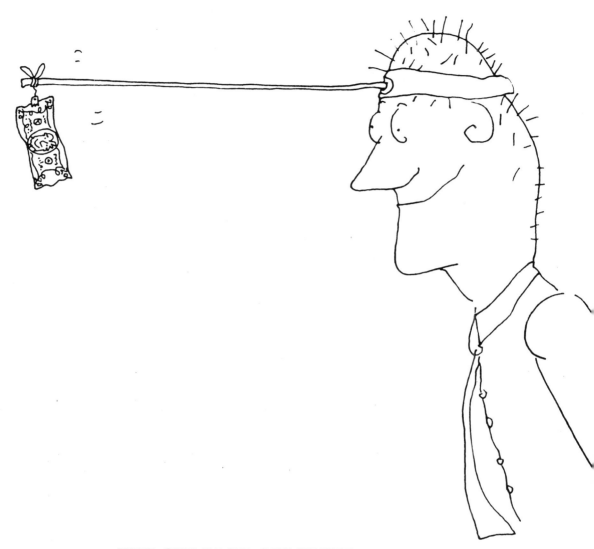

THE GET-RICH-QUICK KIT

It works on the same principle
As the carrot on a stick.
It builds incentive and ambition,
And before you know it, you're extremely rich.

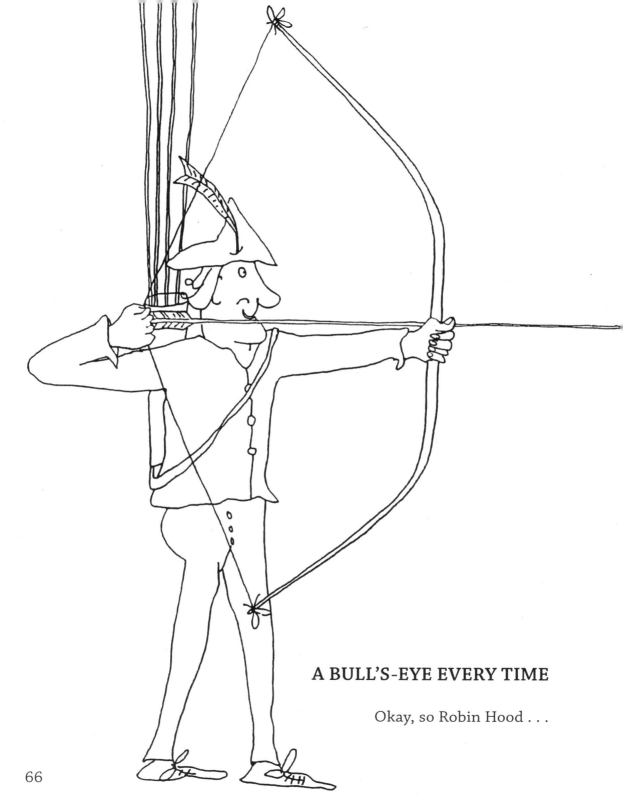

A BULL'S-EYE EVERY TIME

Okay, so Robin Hood . . .

was pretty good.

But how could he be bad,

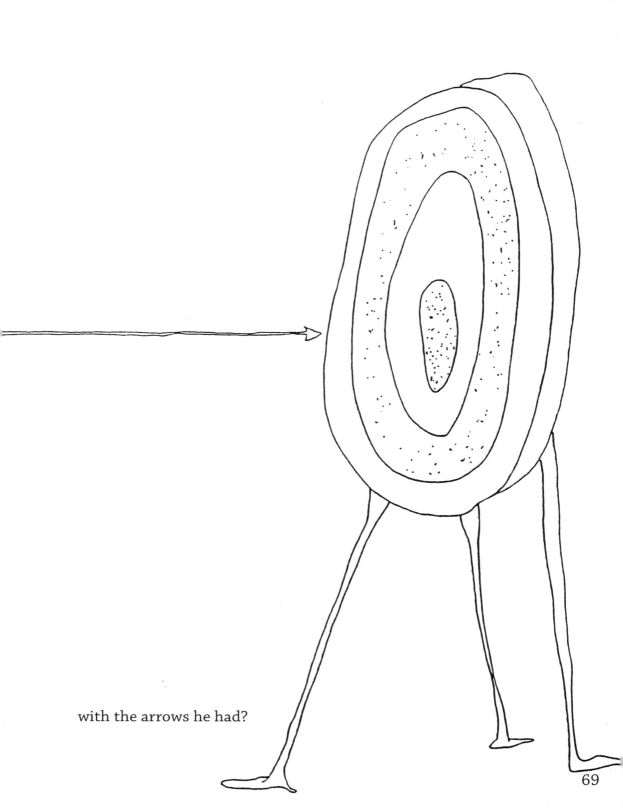

with the arrows he had?

LUCKY ESCAPE

I thought the world was being attacked last night,
When a squadron of flying saucers came into sight.
But luckily it turned out to be instead
A fleet of huge but harmless galactic fried eggs.

71

NEW ICE SKATES

Fifty-five days and nights ago,
The weather was so cold
That it made the seven seas
Stop ebbing and flowing and freeze.
"Yippee!" I cried. I couldn't wait
To put on my scarf and my new ice skates
And to glide and slide on the frozen blue
That glittered out there like a priceless jewel.
And for fifty days and fifty nights,
I skated over that shiny ice
Until I came to distant shores
And realized . . . oh-oh, the ice had thawed!
Yes, before me lay a sandy beach,
A paradise that I had reached.
A blue and beautiful lagoon sea
With palm trees swaying in the breeze.
And there I was, and here I am,
Stranded in this sultry land,
Looking completely out of place
In a wooly scarf and brand new skates.

DUMB DOOR

Ali Baba stood before the door.
"OPEN SESAME!" he roared.
But the door remained
   quite tightly closed.
It wasn't listening, he supposed.
"OPEN SESAME!" again he roared,
Yet still his order was ignored.
Umm . . . they were the right words,
   he was sure.
Yes, right words, but . . .
   er . . . wrong door!

QUARNUUG RURDDLE URID SWIT?
(How's your iguana today?)

I've invented a new language
Shall I teach you it?
OK. Let's start with
Quarnuug rurddle urid swit?
Do you like the sound of it?
That means: How's your iguana today?
Well, maybe that's not such a useful phrase.
How about: Yukrimp churbop duffuff jee.
That's: The sky has fallen in the sea.
What do you mean, "No, it hasn't."
I know it hasn't—
But it might: Hust kug cipot fig bog shgine.
(Never kiss a porcupine.)
You can see how handy this might be
If you're really in a squeeze,
Where no one around you speaks your lingo,
Then, hey, presto! Bingo!
You can say, "Fud smeek ji ow oops grimma yosha?"
(Does anyone here have a waffle washer?)
What? How many people speak this language?
(You mean: Toog frume kwip soo zoop swabkaag?)
Well, there's me and then there'll be you,
But soon they'll be teaching it in every school,
And before you can say moopzorbit
The whole world will be speaking it.
What? You think I've lost my marbles?
I'm cuckoo, round the twist?
Well, you just wait a bit
Till everyone's chatting in it,

And yes, you can laugh at me,
But I'll laugh last, you'll see.
'Cause when someone comes up to you and says,
"Xeeno obb dod goo quisquate?"
Don't ask me to translate!

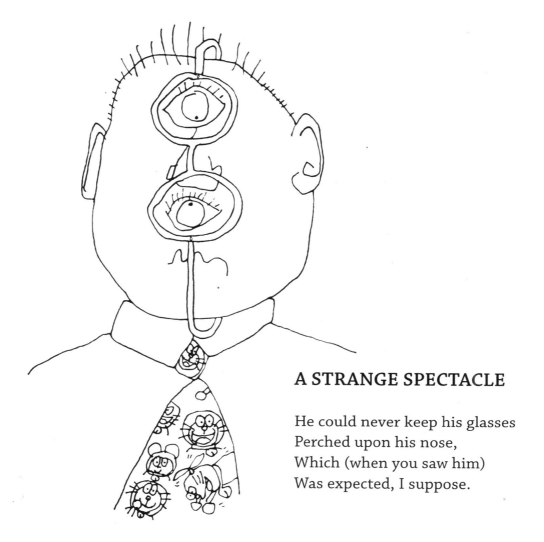

A STRANGE SPECTACLE

He could never keep his glasses
Perched upon his nose,
Which (when you saw him)
Was expected, I suppose.

LOST IN THE JUNGLE GYM

When I climbed into the jungle gym,
I found myself in a fantastic world
Where the sky was covered with squawking birds,
Where monkeys chattered and wild beasts roared.
Nasty snakes slithered across the floor,
And squinty eyes looked through the leaves,
All winking hungrily at me.
Where mosquitoes were the size of crows,
And slimy stuff squeezed through my toes.
Great sticky slugs dropped down my back,
And giant frogs smiled and spat
Right in my ear, and I couldn't sit down
For all the porcupines on the ground.

AND IT WAS THEN . . .

That I saw those dragon tracks.
And I knew that any moment I'd be attacked
By some flame-throwing monster dressed in scales
Twice the size of a killer whale!
And I ran and I ran through the jungle gym,
But the more I ran, I was trapped within.
Entangled in creepers and tigers' tails—
Chased by a herd of kid-eating snails.
And I fell in a swamp of chewing-gum mud,
And I wrestled with alligators in the sludge,
And I chopped my way through the jungle leaves,
The thicket of thorns . . . (Oh, what a terrible dream!)
Until I fell out into the playground at last.

Phew! I've never been so happy to be back in class!

P.S.
If you think that the jungle gym
Is a wild and dangerous thing,
Then try playing in the quicksand pit
Or on the supersonic swings.

PERFECT VISION

They say that bats don't use their eyes
But are guided by high-pitched squeaking.
But I think maybe they do some cheating
And do a bit of peeking.

FAST ASLEEP

When I find it hard to sleep
I count cheetahs instead of sheep.
Why cheetahs, you ask?
Well, I get to sleep twice as fast.

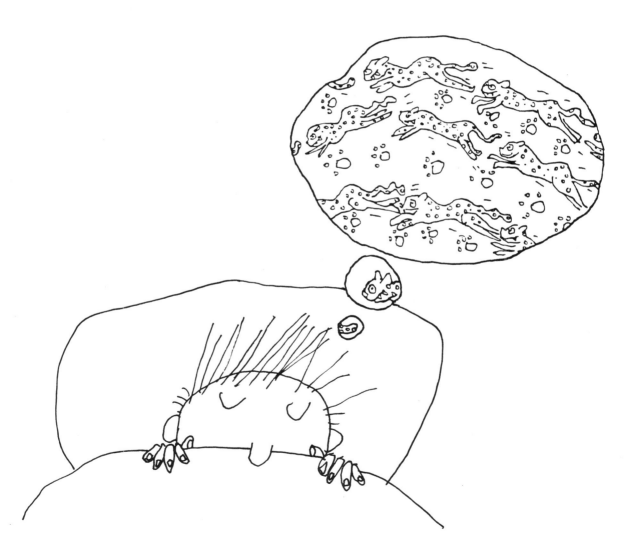

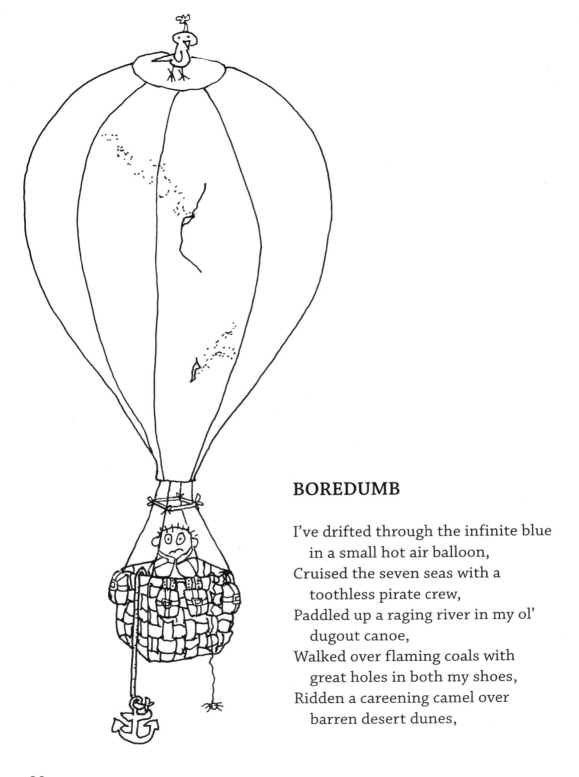

BOREDUMB

I've drifted through the infinite blue
    in a small hot air balloon,
Cruised the seven seas with a
    toothless pirate crew,
Paddled up a raging river in my ol'
    dugout canoe,
Walked over flaming coals with
    great holes in both my shoes,
Ridden a careening camel over
    barren desert dunes,

Roller-skated all the way from my house to Timbuktu,
Sat with starving cannibals and shared their steaming stew,
Whistled fearless tunes while skipping down the
    Valley of Doom.
I've wrestled with argumentative alligators and
    disagreeable dragons, too,
And swooped across the heavens on a stolen witch's broom.
But still, but still, it's only noon—
Now what am I going to do?
I hope life's more exciting this afternoon!

WISHFUL THINKING

I know the world
Goes round and round,
But sometimes I wish
It would go up and down.

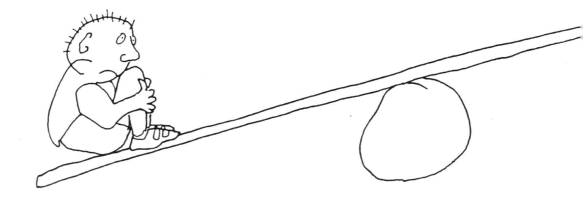

NATURAL CASH

My father is always saying,
"Money doesn't grow on trees."
So why's he in the garden
Checking all the leaves?

WRONG HOUSE, WRONG MOUTH

Last night the tooth fairy
Came and took my tooth,
Which surely did surprise me
'Cause it wasn't even loose.

THE SILENCE OF OUR CLASS

The silence of a pin upon a seat,
The silence of parrots when they screech,
The silence of wolfman's midnight howl,
The silence of a flick with a nice wet towel.
The silence of a siren and an electric saw,
The silence of a lion's thunderous roar,
The silence of an elephant on your toe,
The silence of a nose when it's blown.
The silence of a bee sting on the behind,
The silence of babies when they cry,
The silence of a toothache in your mouth,
The silence of life in the monkey house.
The silence of shouting down a well,
The silence of an ear-piercing, blood-curdling yell,
The silence of tin cans in the wind,
The silence of relief when the school bell rings.
The silence of a hammer breaking glass,
This is the silence of our class.

BOOK JUICE

I'm constantly being told
By those who seem to know,
"When you drink from the Well of Life,
You have to be thirsty for knowledge."
So, perhaps if I put my books in the blender,
Added a dash of lemon or orange,
I could sip great wisdom through a straw
And be smart forevermore.

ETERNAL YOUTH

I have this special cream
For getting rid of wrinkles and lines.
Unfortunately, it removes your nose and ears.
Otherwise, it's just fine.

WALKING, TALKING
TREASURE HOUSE

I'm not like you, I'm dripping in
    jewels.
I've pearls wrapped around my neck,
I've fistfuls of rings—
The envy of kings—
The plunder of the old Aztecs.

I'm a walking, talking treasure house,
I'm a living Aladdin's fable.
Dangling emeralds
From my ears
And a ruby in my navel.

Oh, I'm rich, so very, very, very rich—
Not just a little bit.
But obscenely, queenly,
Meanly rich,
Very, very rich.

I've got a chest full of chunks of burning gold,
Pieces of eight, old doubloons.
Everything of mine
Glitters and shines—
My room's like Cleopatra's tomb.

I've got pockets full of assorted cash:
Lira, pounds, and francs.
Yards and yards
Of credit cards,
And I own a dozen banks.

Oh, I'm rich, so very, very, very rich—
Not just a little bit,
But serenely, supremely,
Extremely rich,
Very, very rich.

I went out shopping and bought the world.
I own a couple of stars.
I've a collection of clouds
With silver linings, and
I've a holiday house on Mars.

Oh, I'm rich, I'm rich, so very rich—
But I'm also such a twit!

I've gone and left all my money at home

Er . . . any chance of a loan?

A BOTTLE OF FEELINGS

He bottled up his feelings
And threw them in the sea
With a note that read,
"HELLO, OUT THERE, IT'S ME."

Years later the bottle
Reached a far-off shore
Where a young girl found it,
And out the feelings poured.

She read the note within—
Who can this really be?
Whose are all these feelings
That have sailed across the sea?

But as it was so hot,
She really couldn't stop
Putting the bottle to her lips
And drinking every drop.

Umm . . . how sweet the feelings—
She wished there were some more.
So off she went in search of bottles
Up and down the shore.

Of course, you're thinking . . .
What about poor "he," he can't be just ignored.
She drank up all his feelings!
What did she do that for?
I don't know (but she found no more).
And he didn't care, I'm sure—'cause he had no feelings at all.

SMELING B

i cant spel CRIS AN THUM MUMS
but i can smel um—
smel um a hundrid myulz away
smel um tday frum yestiday
smel strorberis frum ten thowzand feat
smel dinna that a spanyud eets
smel spysez frum the china see
smel a peece ov peetsa in itale
smel smelee camulz in timbuktoo
smel chickin cury in catmandoo
smel cofee cumin frum kilimanjiro
smel qwite a pong ov un indiun rino
smel lots ov snifs and lots ov wifs
cos i woz born aqiped wiv this
a noze that goze and goze and goze
yeahr, the bigest hoota that i no
ov corse, wen wee hav speling tests
im not so gud, I ges
but if wee had a smeling test
i no eyed be the best!

SONIC SUE

When Sonic Susan sings,
She's like an angel (without the wings).
And from her birdlike throat
There comes a lovely note
That reaches such high frequencies
It takes the leaves right off the trees—
And windows break,
And babies wake,
And dogs yelp out in fear,
And anyone who's standing near . . .
Oh dear, oh dear, oh dear!

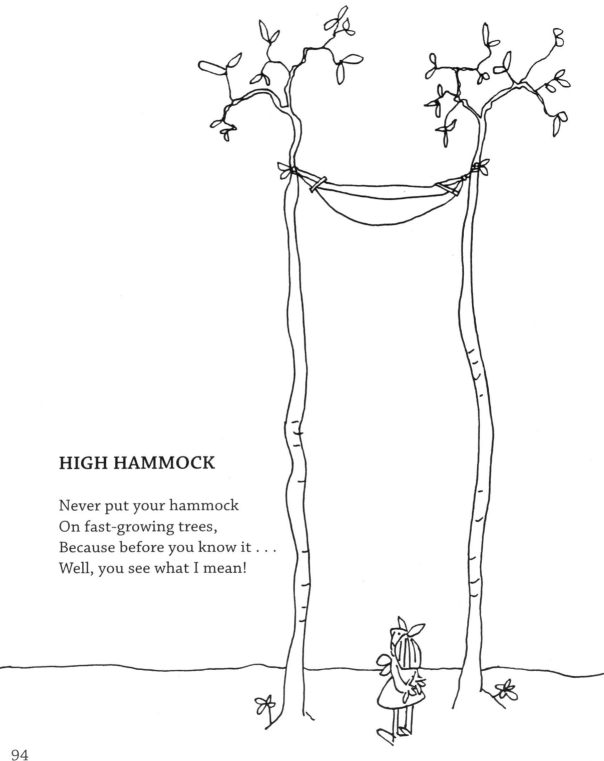

HIGH HAMMOCK

Never put your hammock
On fast-growing trees,
Because before you know it . . .
Well, you see what I mean!

94

TRAVELING LIGHT

The latest fashion for travelers
Is a suitcase with wings
That flies on ahead of you,
So you don't have to check in a thing.

LIGHT-HEADED

I'm glad we're not like plants
That grow towards the light,
'Cause if we were, I know for sure
We wouldn't be a pretty sight!

BEFORE

AFTER

HOT NEW HAIRCUT

The sun's just had a haircut,
A short back and sides,
So if the day's a little dull
That's the reason why.

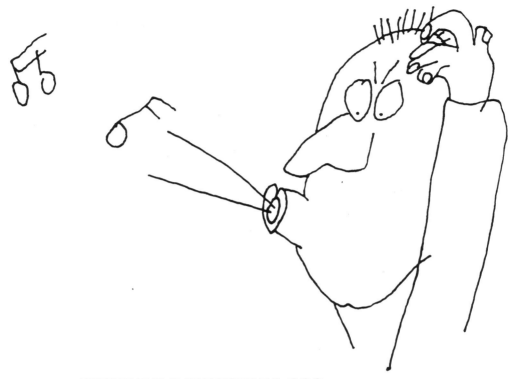

WHERE DO WHISTLES GO?

When a whistle leaves my lips, like so,
Where does it go? That's what I'd like to know.
Is it the same place where cat meows go,
And the noise of noses when they're blown?
Is it where the scratching on blackboards ends up,
With the scraping of forks across a million plates?
Somewhere reserved for the slamming of doors
And the splintering sound when a window breaks?

Is this where whistles go? Well, is it? Is it?
'Cause if it is, that's the last place I want to visit!

METRIC MARY'S MEASURING MADNESS

Metric Mary has a ruler,
Thinks she's Einstein, but cooler.
But really she's just measuring mad—
She's got Measuring Madness, real bad.

She's measured her pencils, eraser, her pen,
Measured the classroom from end to end.
She's measured herself from shoe to neck,
Measured the dimensions of every desk.
She's measured her textbooks,
    the blackboard, the chalk,
All of the dinner hall's knives and forks.
She's measured the corridor,
    her locker door,
Measured the pictures on the wall.
She's measured the playground
    and the great school gates,
Measured the . . . but wait!
Even if she is Einstein,
    but cooler,
Shouldn't someone
    take away that ruler?

A ROCKY RELATIONSHIP

Somewhere along the road of life
He met his beautiful wife.
And though it was a rocky marriage,
From morning until late at night
They never once had a fight.

OPTIMIST

I'm training my dog to do my homework.
So far, he's not very good,
But I'm sure he could get better—
He could! He could! He could!

THE MARRYING MOOD

When I was six years old
And in the marrying mood,
I asked Annie and Jenny
And Deirdre and Sue,
"D' y' wanta get married today?"
And all of 'em said, "OK."

But Annie and Jenny and Deirdre
Went and ran away,
And Sue said, "If I get married,
What have you got to trade?"

"Well, y' can 'ave my bestest marble,
And I suppose my new pet snail,
A real moon rock, a football sticker,
And a magic rusty nail."

Then standing in the sandpit,
With Billy Snodgrum as the priest,
I gave Sue my marrying smile
Through my missing teeth.

"Do y' wanta marry me?
If y' do say 'I Do.'"
"Nah, I've changed my mind, I
    don't.
It's too difficult to choose

Between you . . .

And Brian and Andrew
And Philip and John . . .
How can I marry
Just one?"

So as you can guess,
I didn't get wed
But played cops and robbers
Instead.

LITTLE DARING DOREEN

O what a sight to see,
Little Daring Doreen,
Diving into a cup of tea
From the top of the apple tree.

A somersault, a corkscrew turn,
A swallow flying free.
A jackknife, a backward flip,
Half twist and wheeeeeee . . .

GRAVITY ON MY GRADES

My teacher says that gravity
Helps to keep things down.
So when it comes to grades,
There must be lots around.

Down

Down

Down

Down

Into that cup of tea.

Umm . . .
   rather her than me!

THE SHERIFF OF SPOOKS

Howdy, I'm the sheriff
Of this dusty old ghost town,
And I can tell you one thing now—
I've the easiest job around.

Since all the folks ran out,
Sure, it's a little bleak.
I can walk these streets for weeks,
And never a soul I'll meet.

That is . . . except the Bloody Bandit
With a bullet between his eyes,
And the Horrible Headless Cowboy
Who goes looking for his smile.

There's the Terrible Flying Tomahawk
That's dripping with slimy goo,
And the Ghoulish Gunslinger with his bony fingers
Who passes right through you.

There's Screaming Saloon Sally
With her skeleton-slim Masked Man,
And ghostly gamblers still cheating at cards
Even though they've got no hands.

Now, of course, I know you're thinking,
"What? The easiest job around!
You wouldn't get me within a million miles
Of that creepy old ghost town."

But really it's a sheriff's dream
Keeping order in these streets.
There's never a holdup or a barroom brawl—
For a sheriff it's such a treat!

For you might be surprised to hear
That ghosts and ghouls and their spooky friends
Are just as frightened of us
As most of us are of them.

So it's not that I'm big and bold
(Although I'd like to think I am).
It's not that I've nerves of steel,
That I'm some sheriff superman.

It's just that I have this little trick
(That I'm sure will make you smile)—
All I have to do is simply say,

"BOO!"

And everyone runs a mile.

COMPETITION IN CLASS

As you might expect,
To become the teacher's pet
You really, *really* have to compete,
But how many apples can a teacher eat?

So this morning I thought I'd try
Something a little different instead.
That's why I wrote the teacher a note,
And this is what it said:

"Teacher, how about a brand new Cadillac—
One with a swimming pool in the back?
Or a great big house in Beverly Hills,
And a suitcase full of dollar bills?"
(I thought, if that doesn't work, nothing will!)

And of course, it did.
(Hey, who's a clever kid?)

But it's an expensive business
Being the teacher's pet.
Still, there are some things
You just have to do,
Although I'm hoping now
That my teacher won't mind
If I give him an

IOU.

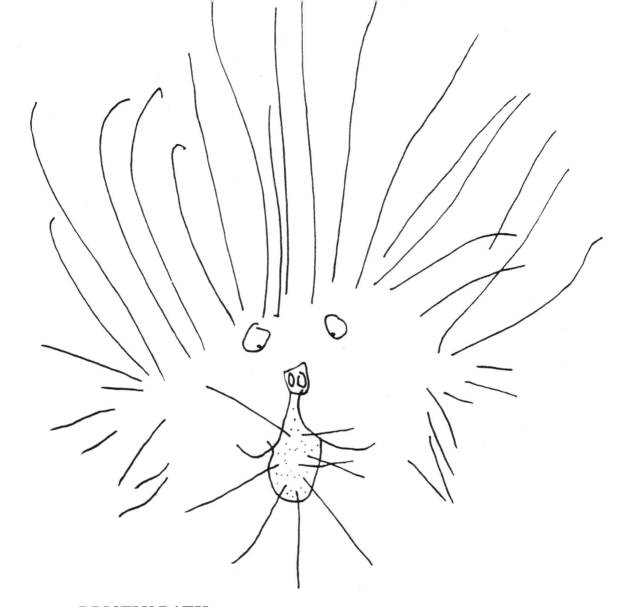

BRISTLY BATH

Like the cat, the porcupine
Bathed with its tongue,
But it soon found out from experience
That this wasn't too much fun.

CHATTERPOT

When I get drunk on tea,
I talk to my ol' teapot
About things that maybe are
And things that are maybe not.
Of grand philosophies,
Of how the world should be,
And I pour out my heart
And it pours out the tea.
But sometimes we can't agree
About what should or shouldn't be,
'Cause the trouble with a pot of tea—
It never talks to me!

THE STORY OF
LITTLE BLUE RIDING HOOD
AND THE BIG GOOD WOLF

Little Blue Riding Hood
Came skipping through the wood,
When to her great surprise
Out jumped the Big Good Wolf.

"Howlo, my little cutie—
What's in the basket, my sweet?
A home-baked apple pie
For a nice old wolf to eat?"

"I've only an iron bar, Mister Wolf,
And a brick in a woolly sock,
But I'm having tea with grandma,
So I really should be off."

    "Whoa, there!" said the Big Good Wolf,
    And he drew himself right up,
    And he huffed and he puffed and
        He puffed and he huffed,
      And pretended to be tough.

      Then he swallowed up the brick,
      Chewed up the woolly sock,
      And wolfed right down the iron bar,
      Which gave "Blue" quite a shock.

"I thought you were supposed
   to be good?"
Queried Little Blue Riding Hood.
"Not that good," Wolf said.
"Anyway, I thought you were
   supposed to be red!"

"Oh, that's my silly sister.
I didn't know you knew her.
I'm not like her at all,
I'm naughtier and bluer."

"But Wolfy, look what you've done!
You've eaten up my brick!
You've gobbled up my iron bar—
There's wool around your lips."

"Oh, I'm terribly sorry, my dear,
But why the bar and the brick?
Why the woolly sock?
They've made me rather sick."

"Well," smiled Miss Hood,
"That'll teach you not to be good.
My mother said, 'Be careful, Blue,
When walking through the woods.

Beware of the good that's bad
And take your mother's advice,
For not everything in the woods
Is cute and sweet and nice.

So take this iron bar
And this brick in your father's sock,
And if you meet a wolf
Knock his block right off.'"

"A-ha!" said the Big Good Wolf,
"Then it's too late for that now.
They're all down here inside."
And he laughed and growled and howled.

But Little Blue Riding Hood,
A twinkle in her eye,
Looked up at the howling wolf
With a pretty, sugary smile.

And on that woodland path
She opened up her

HUGE
HUGE

mouth

And gobbled up the Big Good Wolf,
Then skipped to grandma's house.

A PACKET OF ALPH-ALPHABET

I sowed an A and up it came.
I planted a B—a shoot of green.
I ploughed in Cs, some Ds, a speck of E,
The very best of flowering F.
And while the Gs put forth their leaves,
I dug in a little h, an I, a J, a spot of K,
And watered them every day.
I scattered some L and M, a grain of N, a few of O.
I tended them with my hoe and hoped that they would grow.
I popped in a pinch of P, a handful of quality Q,
And in keeping with the golden rule, I added a little u.
I sprinkled in some R and S until it was time for T.
(Oh, U really can't believe how tiring sowing can be!)
I plucked out all the weeds, I raked in a row of Vs,
A small wee w, a little x, and then, at last, I took a rest.
I stretched myself upon the ground.
I listened to my growing sounds,
And as they all grew over me,
Y, I closed my eyes
And went to ZZZZZZZZZZZZ . . .

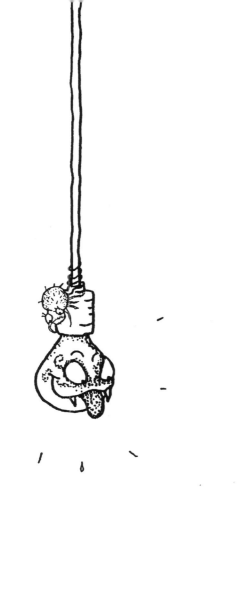

OH DEAR, I FEAR . . .

I'm frightened
Of the dark,

So the light
Stays on
All night.

But now
I'm afraid
I might,

Be frightened
Of the light.

O what a pickle!
O what a stew!
O what a dither!
O what to do?

IT'S A WEIRD WORLD AFTER ALL

The sight—very weird.
In the sky—a flying ear.
And why such speed?
Why indeed? Why indeed?

Was it something over that distant horizon
That it was speeding on to hear?
A festival of wondrous sounds,
Pure luxury to the ear?

Or was it speeding away
From nasty noises, a terrible din?
So I shouted out, "Hey, where are you going?
Hey, where've you bin?"

But what was so very weird
Was that that silly flying ear
Either took no notice
Or just didn't hear.

But kept on flying across the sky
Like some wild and crazy bird,
Leaving me down there to ponder
The mysteries of the world.

Ah, the mysteries of the world . . .

(Of course, it was a foolish thing for me to do,
To shout up into the sky,
For when I think of it now,
How could an ear reply?)

MY MARVELOUS MOBILE

Today, we all made mobiles
To decorate the classroom ceiling.
We were told to be creative:
"Be imaginative. Use your feelings."
We had to have a special theme,
Like the stars and planets in space,
Or cut-out pictures of flying food
Entitled "My Favorite Tastes."

So I sat there deep in thought,
Wondering what to do,
Wanting to be clever,
And startlingly new.
Until it suddenly came to me—
"My Best Friends" would be my theme,
For all I needed was some thread,
Some wire and glue.
And a few very personal things, too.
Like Margaret Blipey's braces
And Colin Winkleberry's shoes.
Richard Trollop's brand new pen,
And that wristwatch of Mary Lou's,
Mickey Mocket's baseball bat.
Gloria Ruffty's horn-rimmed specs,
Ribbons from a dozen ponytails,
Plus last night's homework and a few old tests.
Pencils, erasers, rulers,
Billy Watkin's dinosaur book,
A sandwich from Lucy Peedle's lunch box,
And a pile of other things I took
To make my fabulous masterpiece

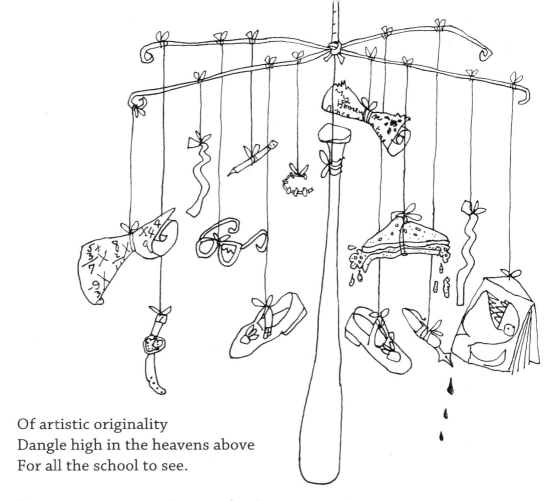

Of artistic originality
Dangle high in the heavens above
For all the school to see.

But as you can guess, it caused quite a commotion,
With lots of reaching up and leaping,
Standing on tippy-toes on top of desks,
With a chorus of shrieking and weeping.

Oh, but undoubtedly it was worth it—
Look! It's something you can almost worship.

So, thank you, friends for your support and aid,
For helping in your little ways.
For eventually when I get my grade,
I bet it'll be an A.

FAILED FASHION

He rather hoped he'd start a fashion—
Mustaches on the chin.
But to his disappointment,
No one copied him.

THE SILLY SEA SONGS
OF THE FLYING FISH

The pet shop said it would sing to me
All the songs of the seven seas,
But all it does is fly round and round
Making weird little gulping sounds.

123

THE ARTIST, HENRY HAMMERHEAD

With my little hammer and chisel
From a mountain I carved a man,
But when I stood back and looked at him,
His head was too big, his neck too thin.
So I chipped and I chiseled once more
And carved a gigantic door.
But the door it had no key,
So it was no use to me.
So I hammered and hammered again
And made a great rock hen.
But the hen it would not lay,
So I hammered again all day
And carved a beautiful egg
The size of an elephant's head.
But the egg I could not eat,
So I smashed it at my feet
With my hammer
That hammered
And hammered
And hammered
And hammered
And hammered
Until that egg was dust
....
....
....

Then I took my little brush
And swept the mountain up.

TRUE LOVE

"Here, darling, I've picked you a rose."
"But that's not a rose, it's a nose!"
"Oh, so it is, but don't feel blue,
When I picked it I was thinking of you."

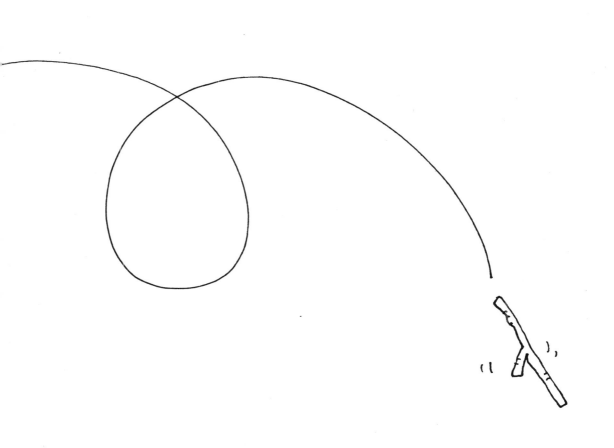

SMART SNAIL

I've trained my pet snail
To go and fetch a stick.
I might have to wait a bit,
But he's very good at it.

AN AMAZING ACT OF INVISIBILITY

"I'm learning to juggle air."
"Juggle air? That's very rare."
"Yes, and especially difficult too,
When you can't see anything there."

UNFORGIVEN

It's not fair!
No one seems to care.
I'm the one who's blamed,
Who gets the bad name.
Yes, I know I put it on the chair,
But I did say,: "No! No!
DON'T SIT THERE!"

Yet no one seems to care
That you squashed my prickly pear!

129

THE SHOP OF SHOCKS

In the Creepy Crawly Shop of Shocks,
You can't imagine what they've got in stock—
Boxes full of bloodshot eyes, warts for a witch's nose,
Three-inch pointed fingernails, and hairy ogre toes.
Bottles of red and runny stuff that's labeled "Dracula Pop,"
And cans of slime 'n' bubbling brews 'n' sticky goos and lots
Of werewolf howls 'n' creaking doors, 'n' squeaky vampire bats.
Brand new broomsticks, wailing cats 'n' a dangerous flying axe.
A row of heads that wink at you, a severed hand that waves,
Bags of sweets in shapes of skulls that are
    "ONLY FOR THE BRAVE."
A set of Shivers for the spine, a shelf of Ghostly Moans,
And posters of your Favorite Fiends, an assortment of
    whitened bones.
Haunting Powder, Spooking Dust, a talking skeleton,
And a notice written in what looks like blood:

FUN FOR ALL THE YOUNG

I was in the Creepy Crawly Shop of Shocks just the other month,
And I'd picked out a Fog-Flavored Lollipop and some Grave Drops
   to munch.
I took them to the counter, where the owner, a weird little man,
Gave me a drippy, fangy smile and reached out a hairy hand.
"Do y' like my 'Orrible 'Ouse?" he said. "My little Shop of Shocks?"
I couldn't move my lips but showed I d-d-did with a t-t-trembling nod.
"Goooood," he said, and his eyes glowed red, and a chill went though
   my heart.
"Well, if that's the case, you should come back sooooon—

But come back after dark."

COMPLAINT

This skipping rope's not working—
I should take it back to the store.
It hasn't skipped at all,
So I'd like to get one more.

DANGEROUS DRIVING

D' y' wanna pass y' driving test?
Here, start with a wheel. I think that's best.
It's a good beginning, but for heaven's sake
Remember you still don't have any brakes!

BAD BOY

I dreamt I'd been captured
By three-eyed Zoglabites
Who only ate their victims
When they were nice and ripe.

They were munchyaupetarians,
And like melons and like plums,
They'd squeeze you between their fingers
And their twenty-five sticky thumbs.

Now, when they did this to me,
All I could do was blush.
My head, it turned bright red,
And they screamed, "He's ripe enough."

Well, they sprinkled me with sugar
And dipped me in chocolate sauce,
And their mouths started drooling.
They were terribly rude and coarse.

And one then picked me up—
Snap! Snap! Just like that.
He took a bite and licked his lips,
But he missed me and got my hat.

"Yuck! This one tastes like cardboard and muck!
I tell y', this boy's bad!
But never mind, there's plenty more.
Let's eat his mom and dad."

*   *   *   *   *   *

134

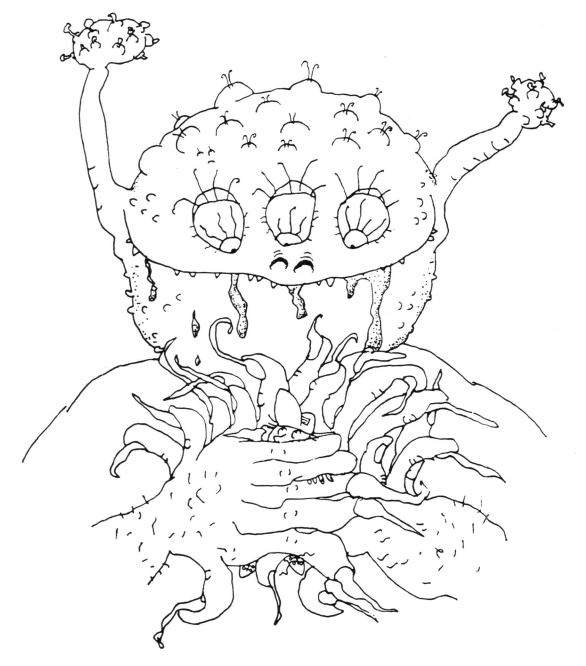

Hey, I can't help it if dreams come true.
Anyway, what could I do?
I'm sorry, mom. I'm sorry, dad.
But it's sometimes good to be bad.

AN EXAGGERATION

My mom says, "TV's not good for you.
It's really bad for your eyesight."
But I think she's exaggerating.
My eyes are perfectly all right!

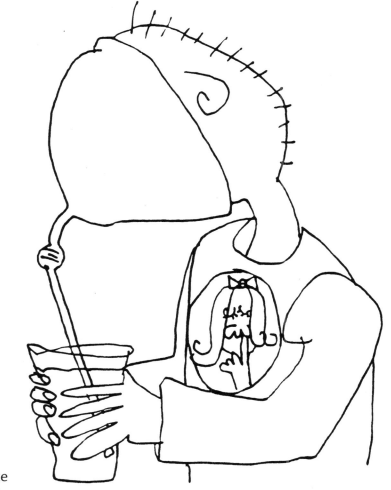

STRAW JAWS

Straws are kinda cute
Sticking in your milk or juice.
But hidden beneath that cuteness
Are creatures, wild and ruthless.

So beware, I say,
For there'll come a day,
When you take a strawberry shake,
Lick your lips and take a sip . . .

It's then when a straw will attack,
And suddenly . . . sip back!

A SOCK IN THE NOSE

THIS IS THE TALE OF ONE STRIPED SOCK
THE SOCK THAT WAS   NEVER WASHED
THAT BELONGED TO PEG-LEG   PHEEEEW
THE   WORST   OF   A   PIRATE   CREW
WHO REFUSED TO TAKE THIS ONE SOCK OFF
UNTIL THE DAY HIS SHIP GOT LOST
AND THERE HE WAS OFF UNKNOWN SHORES
SURROUNDED BY   THE   JU-JU   JAWS
A TRIBE OF   STARVING   CANNIBALS
WHO DIDN'T LIKE THE TASTE OF WOOL
BUT LICKED THEIR LIPS 'N' THEN TUCKED IN
AND THREW THE STRIPED SOCK IN THE BIN
A GOON-GOON BIRD WAS FLYING BY
AND IN THE BIN THE SOCK IT SPIED
SO SWOOPING DOWN AT LIGHTNING SPEED
IT CARRIED THE SOCK INTO THE TREES
AND THERE IT STAYED FOR A 1000 DAYS
UNTIL   THE   WIND   BLEW   IT   AWAY
ACROSS   THE   OCEAN   TO   A   LAND
WHERE   THERE   SAT AN OLD BLIND MAN
WHO THOUGHT   THE   SOCK   TO BE A RAT
DRAGGED   IN BY HIS PET   GINGER   CAT
HE PICKED IT UP   AND HURLED IT   THROUGH
THE WINDOW   WHERE   A   GIRL   CALLED   SUE
WAS WALKING   WITH   AN   INCREDULOUS LOOK
HER   EYES ALL   BURIED   IN   A   BOOK
UNTIL   THE SOCK CAME HURTLING   DOWN
AND WITH   A SOCKY SORT   OF   SOUND
HIT THE   PAGE   AND   STUCK RIGHT   THERE
THE BOOK   SAILED   UP INTO   THE   AIR
AND DROPPING   DOWN TO   OUTSTRETCHED HANDS
WAS   PASSED FROM HANDS TO HANDS TO HANDS
TO THOSE THAT HOLD THIS BOOK YOU READ
WITH THIS ONE PAGE THAT SMELLS OF CHEESE
AND STILL THE SOCK REMAINS UNWASHED
THE ONE TO TAKE YOUR NOSE
RIGHT   OFF!

THE KARATE KID

The Karate Kid is good—
Can slice right through a plank of wood,
Can punch a huge hole in a wall
And never flinch at all,
Can break in two a pile of bricks
A hundred layers thick,
And chop down towering old oak trees
With swift and graceful ease.
So if you meet him, try somehow
Not to shake his hand—just bow.
Though, if to be polite, you must . . .
Be warned,
    he'll squeeze your hand to dust!

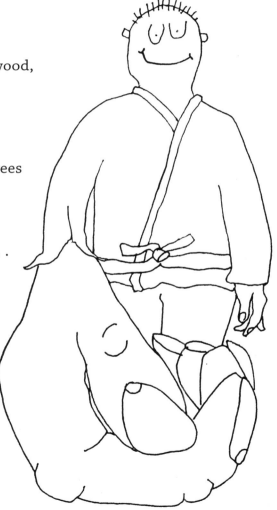

BOUNCING BREAKFAST

Oh, Willy Worm! Oh, Willy Worm!
When will you ever learn?
That by doing your morning exercise
On your little trampoline,
For bright and early birds
You're very easily seen.

Oh, Willy Worm! Oh, Willy Worm!
When will you ever learn?

THE WHOPPER THAT WASN'T

I'm fishing fo
                    r
                    r
                    r
                    r
                    r
                    r
                    r
                    r
                a whopper, a showstopper of a fish,
To make 'em gawk and goggle and go, "Wow, how I wish
I'd caught that one! It weighs a ton! Hey son, look what you've done!
You've caught the biggest fish that's ever graced a dish!"

I've sat here by this river f

                    i
                    i
                    i
                    i
                    i
                    i
                    i
                shin' for that fish
And caught everything you'd wish for except that whoppin' fish.
I've hooked a sofa, snagged an oven,
Pulled up kettles by the dozen.
Hauled out bookshelves, TVs, beds,
Horseshoes, buckets, iron and lead.
Wicker armchairs, a wooden gate,
Statues, lamp shades, cups and plates.
A motorcycle, socks, and boots.

A grand piano, half a lute.
A couple of frogmen, a submarine,
A steering wheel, a fallen tree.
A yacht, a yak, a Chinese urn,
A bath, a bike, and three stuffed birds.
A top hat, turban, a small canoe,
A treasure chest and two odd shoes.
A telephone, a tennis net,
An iceberg, and a croquet set.
A sieve, a spade, a rusty sword,
  A Hula dancer, a waxed surfboard,
  An office block, a runaway train,
    The whole Himalayan Mountain
      Range.

  But where's that whopper,
    that showstopper,
  That will make 'em gawk and goggle
  And go, "Wow, how I wish
    I'd caught that one!
  It weighs a ton! Hey son,
    look what you've done!
You've caught the biggest fish
  that's ever graced a dish."

Ah, fishing's such a bore.
I don't think there's anything worth
  catchin' in this river at all!

143

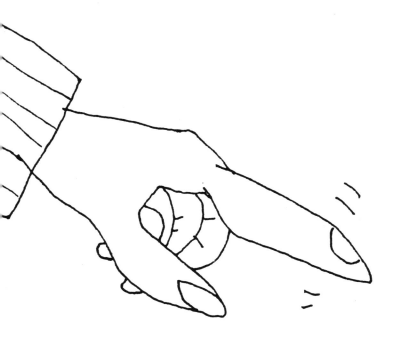

SLIPPER TRAINING

I put my slippers by my bed
And said, "Good slippers! Stay!"
But in the morning those naughty slippers
Had gone and slipped away.

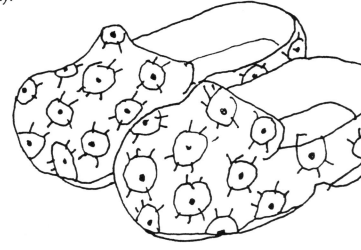

DOGPOX

Spotty, you're covered in spots!
Spotty, are you ill? Spotty, are you hot?
Maybe you've measles or chickenpox?
But as you're not a chicken . . . oh, no! . . . Dogpox!
Umm . . . your tail's still wagging, Spotty,
And your ears are nice 'n' floppy.
You've got the same wet nose,
So you must be okay, I suppose.
It's funny, I'm sick when I'm covered in spots,
But when you are, Spotty—you're not!

GULP GULP

I'm sure my goldfish wants to talk,
But the words just can't get out.
For every time he tries to speak,
He gets water in his mouth.

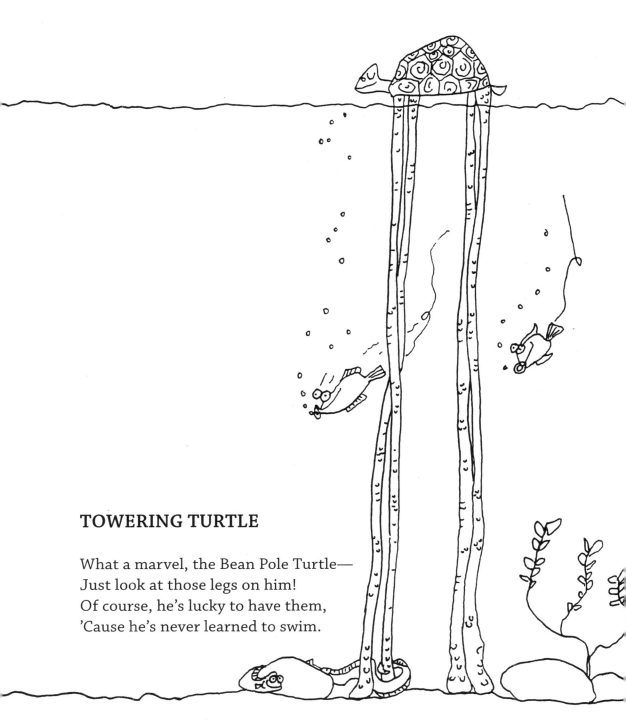

TOWERING TURTLE

What a marvel, the Bean Pole Turtle—
Just look at those legs on him!
Of course, he's lucky to have them,
'Cause he's never learned to swim.

MOUNT MELTY

Ice cream tends to go so quick,
Almost before you can have a lick.
So here's some extra advice of my own—
Always put plenty on the cone!

CHAIR UP

It's
Not
Fair
Said
The
Chair.
Why
Am
I the
One
They always sit on?
So to show the chair
I   cared
I   went
And   bent
At   the
Knees   for
The   chair
To sit   on me

CAT ACT

The Amazing Cat Brothers
　　Balanced cats,
　One on top
　　Of
Each
　Other.
　A marvelous meowing
　Tower of fur—
Oh, see how many cats
　There were.
　　51!
　　52!
　　53!
　　54!
　MORE!
MORE!
　The
　Audience

　　R
　　O
　　A
　　R
　　E
　　D
　　．

　　．

　　．

　　．

　　．
　　．　．　for a tangle of tails, a pile of paws.

151

FEATHERED FATTIES

The Elephant Bird is now extinct—
The world and it have called it quits.
For when it sat upon its eggs,
They all got smashed to bits.

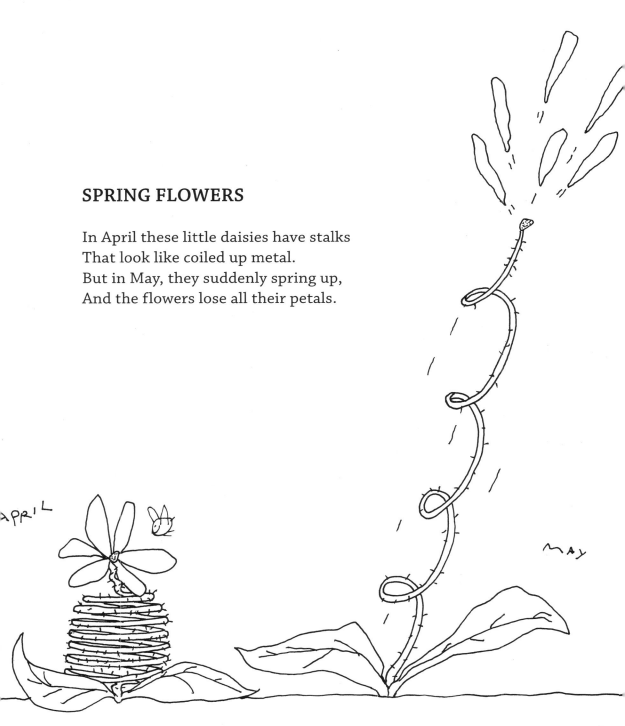

SPRING FLOWERS

In April these little daisies have stalks
That look like coiled up metal.
But in May, they suddenly spring up,
And the flowers lose all their petals.

THE SYMPHONY OF SQUEAKS

I had a singing sofa,
A marvelous musical chair,
And together they made music
Beautiful and rare.

So I put them on the stage
At the Royal Albert Hall,
But to my great surprise
They made no sound at all.

The audience was silent;
Expectantly they stared
At a flowered sofa
And a cozy old armchair.

The curious, the cynical,
Real music lovers too,
Thinking they'd been fooled
Began to hiss and boo.

Where was the soprano singing?
The beautiful and the rare?
But what can you expect
From a sofa and a chair?

Oh, I was so angry!
"Just wait till you get home!
You're in for a good hiding—
Just wait till we're alone."

"Why? Why do that to me?
Tell me! Tell me! Speak!"

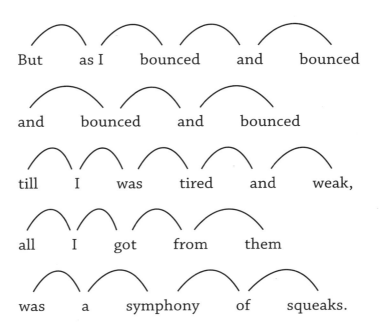

But   as I   bounced   and   bounced

and   bounced   and   bounced

till   I   was   tired   and   weak,

all   I   got   from   them

was   a   symphony   of   squeaks.

THE BOOK OF EVERYTHING

THE BOOK OF EVERYTHING perched there,
A dusty, slumbering exotic bird,

Upon the library's highest shelf,
Above the title TEACH YOURSELF.

The pages packed with figures and facts,
Lists and maps, and this and that—

A thousand thoughts, the wisest minds,
Brilliant ideas on every line.

For all the biggest, smartest brains,
All the geniuses of the day,

Had huddled together head to head,
Refusing to eat or go to bed

Until the book had overflowed
With everything there is to know.

Knowledge at your fingertips,
Lots and lots and lots of it:

Why the sea is soaking wet,
Where suns go when they set.

Why does rain fall down in drops?
What is snow when it's not?

Why's a circle nice and round?
What's the flavor of a cloud?

How to charm an armadillo,
How to soothe a weeping willow.

Where's the longest piece of string,
How to make a bluebell ring.

Who takes sugar in their tea,
How many waves are on the sea.

How to read well in the dark,
How to hypnotize a shark.

This and that and these and those—
All the things that most don't know—

Were stored inside this mammoth book.
But strangely . . . no one even paused to look,

Except one little smarty-pants
By the name of Timothy Banks,

Who wanting to know more and more,
Entered this great library's door,

And climbing up the rickety steps
To where THE BOOK OF EVERYTHING slept,

Reached upon his tippy toes
And took the book, but . . .

O
O
O
O
O
O
O
O
O
O
O
O
O
H
.
.
.

The Weight of Knowledge was too much
For such a tiny Tim to clutch,

And oh, the Egg of Wisdom about to hatch
Made a resounding, awful, squelchy . . .

SPLAT!!!!

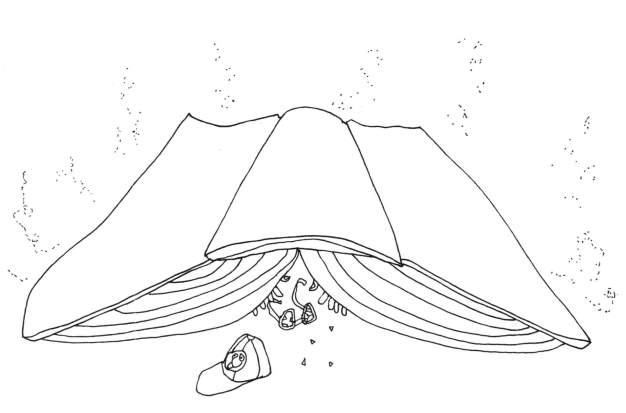

INDEX OF TITLES

162

INDEX OF FIRST LINES

So to close this extra odd oyster
And step back into the wacky world,
O Great One, O goofy guru,
Go preach the wisdumb of the pearls.

OH . . .

Of course tiny Tim survived
And now is exceedingly wise
From burying his head in a thousand books
Far smaller than the one he reached and took.
Though a lesson was learnt, I know—
Never climb up rickety steps alone
And stretch upon tippy toooooooes.
Oh . . . wisdumb comes at a heavy price.
Better to read this book . . . it's light!